MAKING Edited by Katrin Klingan, Nick Houde, and Johanna Schindler, with contributions by Luis Campos, Maria Chehonadskih, Ana Guzmán, Hao Liang, Hu Fang, Elizabeth Povinelli, Sophia Roosth, and Kaushik Sunder Rajan

Making

Edited by
Katrin Klingan, Nick Houde, and Johanna Schindler

Contents

Making

Alphabets systematize abstract representations into analytic instruments. Linguistically, alphabets enable one to break down speech
sounds into forms that are repeatable and recordable. More figura-
tively, alphabet-like structures break down phenomena into discrete
and recombinant series that represent all of its component parts in a
systematic yet open-ended manner.

Amidst a profusion of old and new processes of alphabet making
that echo how the world has been understood, new ways of making
these alphabets operational afford new possibilities for their use. This
entails using them not just as representations but also as tools. These
tools map representations onto physical things in order to manipu-
late them and transform them into unforeseen combinations, going
beyond the scope of what was known about a phenomenon in the
world by testing what could be possible, even if it has yet to exist.

Alphabetic representations such as those used to represent DNA,
for instance, are instrumentalized in order to remake and rearrange
combinations of proteins so that selective traits and genetic expres-
sions are borne, which stretch the realm of what combinations are in
fact biologically possible whether they have occurred in the past or
not. Used in this way, such representations expand what is known by
questioning what *is* with what *could* be.

Thinking about knowledge in this way produces a number of political and ethical questions. If one is no longer shackled to the known
world, then what possible worlds, what possible recombinations, are
worth searching for? Is it simply about making something new and
expanding understanding about the world? Or would such rational-
izations be better off qualified through their various motivations such
as profit, collective wellbeing, discrimination, or justice which have
ultimately guided how the operational knowledge came about?

Starting from these problematics, this book compiles contributions that negotiate values for the world-to-come by making new
possibilities from the fragments of the current one. In this way, the
contributions in the volume not only challenge new alphabets but
also articulate the role value and purpose play in their construction and implementation of past alphabets. It seeks to tackle the
many planetary-scale issues of our time to find common spaces for
negotiation, for finding purpose, and for making forms of life that

seem worth living on this planet between a multitude of perspectives and epistemologies.

The book experiments with the strange pairing of life and form. It attends to how the echo of past articulations of life and form have come to shape the *Making* of a world to come, both actively and passively; producing the technologies and ways of life that underpin the contemporary world. The book takes off from conversations had during the *Life Forms* event at HKW in 2019 by bringing some of their complexities into a new form.

The contributions focus on the issue of making as an active process of responding to countervailing forces made manifest in ways of life, technical systems, and artistic practices. What or who is making what in our world? And how do their instruments and techniques, intentions, and stakes underwrite this process? Similarly, how are these processes transformed by their interactions with other processes and systems in such a way as to produce ambiguity between the natural and technological?

Picking up on the *shan shui* tradition and introducing how it informs techniques of Chinese landscape paintings, Hao Liang's unfoldable work *The Tale of Cloud* serves as a prelude to this volume. The painting in ink uses classic Chinese storytelling techniques to reflect on tensions between scientific inquiry and their relationship to more longstanding forms of subjective inquiry. As each picture element passes over another, a narrative about time and space and the relationship between people and their environment is continuously developing.

In his essay "Shan Shui," author and curator Hu Fang discusses this Chinese painting tradition of the same name. Loosely seen as analogous in form to "landscape" painting in the European tradition, *shan shui* brush-and-ink paintings depict a world in constant interplay of life forces with and as humanity. Fang builds upon the philosophical implications of this tradition to contrast the Chinese vase and Plato's allegory of the cave, both of which offer fundamental insights into how being isolated during the Covid-19 pandemic could be understood. Instead of just observing the play of shadows in the outside world as in Plato's cave, the vase is given form and purpose through its emptiness, just as the impoverished existence of the pandemic can tap into the life-preserving energies and existential needs of humanity as it comes to terms with its place in the world.

Looking at the question of how life is made, Sophia Roosth and Luis Campos dive into the depths of scientific reasoning, laboratory work, and the surprise involved in the construction of life. Revolving around stories from the petri dish to outer space, from the history of science to science-fiction, they discuss whether life emerges in the right circumstances if given the chance and ask: What form can life take and how do you know it when you see it?

The connections between technology, humans, and the environment are discussed from the vantage point of the agency these different elements have in a conversation anthropologist Elizabeth Povinelli, philosopher Ana María Guzmán, and *Info Unlimited* host Reece Cox had for Cashmere Radio around the time of the *Life Forms* event. Their discussion expands on Elizabeth Povinelli's concept of geontopower and demonstrates how the distinctions between life and non-life that are made in the contemporary world have pressing consequences on current modes of governance, policing, and colonial capitalism.

The book concludes with philosopher Maria Chehonadskih speaking to anthropologist and sociologist Kaushik Sunder Rajan, who take on the question "Who and what are we working for?" by discussing their different experiences as academic migrants, and the role political engagement plays in an international academic world. Along with this question, the conversation speaks to how pedagogy is a constant interplay between the contexts and commitments that make and form how knowledge is built upon through the generations.

Katrin Klingan, Nick Houde, Johanna Schindler

Hao Liang
The Tale of Cloud, 2013

Ink and color on silk, handscroll, 45 × 1200 cm
Courtesy of the Artist and Vitamin Creative Space

The Tale of Cloud is a contemporary reflection on the craft and concept of Chinese painting traditions. The piece adapts the detailed brushwork technique of gongbi that was prevalent between the Tang and Song dynasties into an unfolding philosophical narrative in which the artist attempts to recollect the history of human subjectivity—the driving force in the development of scientific inquiry. It digs up the work of preceding traditions and, through their repetition, transforms the perspective toward the body itself, building on the symbols and cosmologies of *shan shui* painting while changing the parameters of time, space, and scale. In this way, it recounts a developing crisis between science and subjective forms of inquiry in the spirit and style of the *shan shui* tradition, in which the role of the human within the world was depicted as codependent, inseparable, and riddled with complexity.

The piece has been scaled down in this book to enable its original unfolding, conveying the sense of narration and temporal flow around which the original is structured.

Shan Shui[1]

An essay on painting as an expressive life practice
and the *shan shui* tradition as a form of situated reflection
on the world

I have watched numerous movies whilst self-quarantining in this room. Yes, today, we have grown accustomed to whiling away our time by binging on video after video. If we imagine the rooms we are currently in as "caves"—akin to the cave in Plato's allegory—then, I wonder, at this very moment, what do we see: shadows of things, or the things themselves?

Two markedly different options are open to us with reference to the "cave": rush with wild abandon toward the light, or remain imprisoned in the dark, all the while with shadows as the intermediary medium between the two. What's interesting from the beginning is that the physical space in which one views a video is akin to a return to the "cave." This experience can only occur under the contrast of darkness and light; it is a liminal state between exposure and concealment. In this way, the experience of watching a video could be seen as a subtle metaphor for our dual human desires: one, to attain enlightenment, and the other, to remain sheltered and protected.

Today, in order to access a plethora of films that will keep a movie fan entertained for a lifetime, one must pay the price: that is, offer one's digital traces unreservedly to data companies free of charge. Consequently, the film fan's whereabouts is also readily available. A ceaseless stream of images satisfies the film fan's curiosity about the

---

1   Translator's note: *Shan shui refers to a Chinese style of painting executed with calligraphy ink and brush that oftentimes focuses on depictions of nature and landscapes. The literal translation of the Chinese words* "山水" *is* "mountain and water," *and these often feature in the paintings. Two characters from the earliest form of the Chinese written script—the oracle-bone inscriptions (甲骨文, pronounced Jia Gu Wen)—form the word shan shui. These characters, which work like pictograms, developed over time into the modern-day Chinese script in use today.*

world and fulfills the yearning. The individual remains trapped by his or her fate as an observer of the "world as projected."

Throughout history, humanity has resorted to various means in pursuit of the "truth." Unlike the spatial attributes of Plato's cave, the Chinese "vase" implies a prototype that has characteristics more aligned to the idea of quantum space. It is not a space that can be measured by the throw of light on it. Rather, the vase's "emptiness" is not only essential to defining its form but also what its existence manifests. Its exterior and interior are enmeshed as one entity, mutually informing and reinforcing each other. It is important to note that the vase does not represent an isolated space. Instead, there is a mutual dependence between the vase and humanity. In fact, the vase itself connotes "peace"; the Chinese word for "vase" and "peace" sound the same phonetically. Thus, the space as inhabited and made manifest by the "vase" brings with it a message for the protection of life.

Throughout Chinese art history, the notion of an intimate relation between art and life has endured throughout the ages. In *Notes from the Painting-Meditation Studio*, Ming Dynasty painter and scholar Dong Qichang wrote: "In the Tao of Painting, the cosmos[2] rests within one's hands. One who appears to be full of life is often blessed with longevity." He went further to provide an example: "Huang Dachi[3] is ninety years old but looks like a child. Mi Youren is over eighty but remains alert as ever. The painting's landscape endows a pleasing sense to them." The latter sentence points to not only how art draws from life's energy by way of immersion and expression, but also how art affects people's lives. In the "habitable and tourable" landscapes of *shan shui* paintings, humans appear to exist in a world replete with an abundance of life force, and this in turn bestows vitality on these said humans.

The Chinese are more inclined toward the term *shan shui* as opposed to "landscape" with reference to the painting style. This stems from the dualism of yin and yang, which refers to one's experience upon being cognizant of the meeting of matter and the universe.

---

2   Translator's note: In Chinese, the word for cosmos (宇宙) indicates the notion of space and time. Dong Qichang's line is related to an earlier point made in the essay with regard to the notion of space inside a vase.
3   Translator's note: The literal translation of the name "黄大痴" is "Big Foolish Huang."

Fundamentally, it is rooted in an outlook that regards the world as comprising diverse elements that mutually relate to and interact with one another. Consequently, this perspective shapes the "abstract" direction that *shan shui* paintings take: the intent is not so much to represent but to realize—and that realization leads to the "image." In this particular view of the universe, "the universe has no aspiration to be anything beyond itself; it is determined by its own growth and change." This is in contrast to the "Western" tradition where "the universe is understood to follow some ultimate scientific laws that determine its development." As such, "the historical model is not to propel towards some predetermined goal, but rather to make the utmost effort to understand the aspects of 'Tao.'"[4] This historiography, while very much challenged in contemporary discourse, is one that has been constantly evolving and transforming, and has gradually become part of the genealogy of Chinese art history. Here, enduring antiquity and eternal renewal are intimately intertwined.

As humanity's sense of perception changes with time, perhaps the topic of *shan shui* painting[5] has passed its golden age. Yet the eclipsed and diffused light that permeates in them gives us an opportunity to escape from the lurid materiality of this era, so that we can lean towards a fundamental time colored with a different hue. Throughout history, Chinese painters have demonstrated a keen understanding of how color and luster play key roles in evoking certain dispersals of light. When talking about illumination in a painting, it is not simply about the presentation of a phenomenon. Rather, light has to do with the sort of energy emanating from the inner nature of things. Perhaps what we should investigate in more depth right now is exactly this: the obscure yet life-preserving creative endeavor that drives *shan shui* paintings. It is resonant to revisit them now, as they seem to answer to some particularly current existential need.

---

4   Wen C. Fong, *Images of the Mind: Selections from the Edward L. Elliott Family and John B. Elliott Collections of Chinese Calligraphy and Painting at the Art Museum, Princeton University*, trans. (to Chinese) by Li Weikun. Beijing: Shaanxi People's Fine Arts Publishing House, 2004, p. 250.
5   If we look at both European paintings related to religious subjects and Chinese *shan shui* paintings related to *"mountain and water"* subjects, we might well discover some commonalities in the human experience of art.

If art hints at the possibility that a world can be realized without desiring an "other"—in contrast to how religions regard "another world," or how philosophy views metaphysical transcendence—then given the imagery within *shan shui* paintings, as well as the invisible force that propels humanity's fate, what relationship will the two share? How will *shan shui* paintings journey with us through our impoverished, dispersed existence?

Translated from the Chinese by Melissa Lim

Making: Reasoning Before the Fact

A conversation about how life is
and how it could be

Sophia Roosth: Given our shared interest in synthetic biology, we have both thought about ways to reason through life and form with reference to construction as a mode of reasoning (following deduction, induction, and abduction). So, one way of posing the question I want to ask is, when you think about the distance that separates life as it is from life as it could be—where does the constructive impulse fit in?

> Luis Campos: I think what I have found so interesting in looking at this question—of what, of how, life could be, of how it may have been, of how it might be in the future, of how we might find it somewhere else—is that these categories of investigation which seem so obviously separate to us sometimes have shared histories. Sometimes people involved in one area are deeply involved in another at the same time; for example, those studying natural life are implicated in the pursuit of engineering life toward forms not found in nature. Our analytical distinction between "life as it is" and "life as it could be" may be a distinction that doesn't exist for our historical actors themselves. When I think of the origin of life, for example—when I think of a moment that has often been referred to as dividing one time from another, of non-life and life—I see the sort of productive conflation of that distinction: the very moment when the origin of life becomes a historical question amenable to experimental investigation is a moment that involves creating something that is almost alive but not quite. The first experiment into the question of the historical origin of life on Earth is in fact an experiment that involves producing in the laboratory something that would have n-1 of the n properties of life, whatever that would be.

SR: Are you thinking, for example, of Friedrich Wöhler's synthesis of urea in 1828 as a putative refutation of vitalism, that is, as a way of demonstrating an abiotic origin of life, or are you imagining something else?

LC: It is often claimed that the artificial synthesis of urea in 1828 was a kind of originary moment in the history of the origin of life, a turn away from vitalism and toward materialism. This claim hasn't stood the test of time or of scholarship. But we often seem to be looking for these kinds of originary moments when we talk about life—even the expression "the origin of life" pushes us this way. If not 1828, then perhaps in 1952, with the Urey-Miller experiment that involved zapping some gases in a container and inorganically producing some amino acids, which many have hailed as the first laboratory experiment into the origin of life.

SR: Miller and Urey did the experiment in 1952, and the following year is the demonstration of the double helix structure of DNA, is that right?

LC: That happened in 1953, that's right, absolutely. But as I thought my way back earlier in time, I encountered a Cavendish Laboratory physicist working in 1904, at the height of the radium craze surrounding the newly discovered radioactive element. He drew on popular understandings to envision a much more intensely radioactive early Earth, thinking about how we might use an experimental set-up to replicate those conditions and try to understand the origin of life. The physicist's name was J. Butler Burke, and he thought, well, the early Earth must have been more intensely radioactive. It must have been a place that had lots of rays flying around, which might have something to do with the creation of life. And since I just said "creation," I think we should also talk about "creation" and "construction" and the way the different words are used; it has everything to do with the meaning of life. Well, Burke envisioned simulating the early-Earth environment in a laboratory to help better understand the origin of life. And so, what he did is he thought he could make life in the test tube, or something that had $n-1$ of the n properties of life. As a physicist, he was entranced by the newfound properties of radioactivity, and he developed an experimental set-up where he put some radium into bouillon, effectively some beef soup, and saw some lifelike cellular forms that began to grow and subdivide over the space of a few weeks. He made images of them with his camera lucida and began to publish his findings. And he argued that these things were "the microbe's ancestors," that these half-radium, half-microbe entities, or "radiobes" as he called them, were being generated by a lively element, radium, that seemed to produce energy which came from nowhere, and as there must have been more radium early on in the history of the Earth, this might explain how life emerged.

What I think is so intriguing about this experiment is that it has an inherent instability to it. When we think about being able to produce something that might crawl out of a test tube or otherwise be "proof of life," we don't often think of the complexities and the criticisms that are made of such claims. Even if something did come crawling out, it could always be explained away as contamination. An experiment is never perfectly clean, or subject to only one interpretation, and certainly not when we are talking about understanding the origin of life. Many critics attacked Burke for having conducted a rather stupid and uninformed experiment—they argued that he had succeeded not in producing life, or even "the microbe's ancestor," but simply some chemical precipitates. And he replied, quite brilliantly, "no, no, if I *had* produced life then you would have thought this was contamination—so it's the very fact that I *didn't* produce life, and I produced something else, something that has n-1 of the n properties of life, and doesn't fit our ordinary expectations of chemistry and chemical behavior, that makes my experiment so interesting and so useful." That argument didn't work. It's a brilliant argument, but it's hard to understand, and it didn't work.

And so, that question of how do we *make* it, how do we *know* it, and how can making something help us understand how nature may have done something is, I think, a series of questions that has been around for a long time.

SR: And the question of how you know it when you see it is something that I've been grappling with as well, because I've been looking at the history of something called a "dubiofossil." I don't know if you're familiar with dubiofossils but, simply, they're fossils that people are dubious about. Earth scientists find a pattern in stone and they think it might be a fossil, but it also might not be. There are plenty of other examples of things that look like they're alive, that take the form of life but in fact aren't. We can talk about going back to protoplasm as a very early example of that. Thomas Henry Huxley, for example, reporting on "Urschleim" (primordial slime) dredged up from the sea floor in the 1860s while laying transatlantic telegraph cables...

It turned out to be just sea slime, even though it got a Latin name. But there are lots of examples of that sort of mistake—of seeing something inorganic and thinking it's a life-form—which continue up until the present. Even if you look at the cover of *Science* or *Nature* as of September 2016, let's say, the announcement that there were 3.7 billion-year-old putative fossils of stromatolites found in Greenland; I suppose, they're currently dubiofossils since there's a lot of argument about them. Subsequently, I've been trying to pay attention to moments where there are these controversies about what counts as a living form and what doesn't. And, in fact, it's actually quite surprising, because I've found that oftentimes the things that people think look least lifelike are more likely to be readily accepted as "true" fossils. Perhaps, then, form is the thing about which scientists are increasingly dubious when it comes to identifying what is really life.

> LC: That makes me think of the Middle Ages when Albert the Great saw what we would understand today to be fossils. In his treatise *De mineralibus,* he sought to explain the curative powers of stones, how water could congeal and create stones along riverbanks, and even how stones could take on particular forms reminiscent of living things because of the influence of the heavens—an astrological account of some geological forms that had a lifelike appearance. Hence, in the Middle Ages, the very clarity of the form was an argument for how life and form were related. Yet today, we've entered into maybe a different place, where to have a clear form is to be suspicious, would you agree?

SR: Yes, right.

> LC: I saw a dubiofossil—now that I have the word—a couple of months ago at the Smithsonian. They showed me an insect

trapped in amber. I looked at it and felt a bit quizzical, like there was something off about it. And then the curators told me it was a prop from the film *Jurassic Park*, and I thought, this is brilliant! I was taken in by it at first, but it was too good, right, it was too perfect, the perfect *form*. Of course, it also resonated with something deep in my childhood of watching this movie and then becoming a historian of biology—what a happy origin story that would be. And as I looked at it, I thought, you know, it's amazing that as I stare at this thing which is a symbol of something, I can be so convinced that it is a fossil, even though I know in my mind that it's not; the form belies the truth in that case.

SR: In my first book, I wrote about what I called "persuasive objects." The claim that I made is this: Synthetic biologists are bioengineers trying to understand what life is or what the limits of life might be. In order to do so, they make simple organisms or even slightly less-than organisms in the laboratory—what you called n-1 of life—such as a bit of genetic material or some other biological system. In the early 2000s, they did so in order to convince themselves that the kinds of criteria or characteristics that they think of as being definitional of life are in fact true. So, a very simplified virus will function as proof of concept or a "persuasive object," because the engineered virus persuades the engineers of what life might be. But given what you just said, one of the things that I should think more about is whether sometimes people are persuaded of things that aren't necessarily so. I don't want to say it's circular, but as a mode of logical reasoning it fastens onto particular characteristics, builds them into substance, and then is convinced of its truth because it has been made.

LC: But sometimes, even unconvincing "dubiofossils" can have a productive effect on research. For example, Craig Venter has talked about how the 1990s controversy over the putative Martian nanofossils found in Antarctic meteorites—forms that were much smaller than any forms of life we were familiar with here on Earth—inspired part of his own interest in minimal genomes and the idea of minimal life. One could observe and wonder at how small life could get morphologically, Venter felt, or one could experiment to figure it out genetically, which he did with his work on "Synthia," or *Mycoplasma laboratorium,* the first synthetic cell with a minimal genome containing just the barest set of genes necessary for life. Wondering about "life as it could be" on Mars was a direct inspiration to wondering about "life as it could be" down here on Earth. And not how we might find it in nature, but how we might *make* it.

SR: Going further, I was thinking about how constructive biology—and constructive reasoning more broadly—could be considered not just as simply constructive but also as demonstrative. These persuasive objects demonstrate something; they show that something could be true by making things. And while I was contemplating the word demonstrative, I recalled that the root of demonstrative is the same as monster, which actually makes sense. So, let me follow this thread for a second: When we talk about what a monster is, we think of something abnormal or something disturbing coming from the laboratory. One way of thinking about the kinds of things that constructive biologists do involves thinking about the word's original meaning, which is a wonder or an omen, a sign of things to come, or a demon. These are things that, because they're abnormal, suggest that something catastrophic is *about* to happen; they are harbingers of a certain kind of future. There are many books about the origins of modern science being tied up with wonderment, but also often with the worry that these kinds of monstrosities are saying something about how the so-called natural order is being disturbed. I was thinking about whether that's another way that we could find an inroad into this topic.

LC: That kind of reference to etymology is a useful technique which we get to use in the humanities all the time. How can words reveal things to us from their aspects and virtues as words? How can we uncover these sometimes-forgotten meanings in how we talk about things today? That monster and demonstration share the same root—that it's wonder, an omen, a demon, all these things at one time. And I think it's an endlessly fascinating method, because you're always able to unfold and find other meanings that are there, but you may not know it until you do the work to uncover them. I've wondered whether that is also how science works at an unconscious level for scientists who are practicing it themselves.

SR: How do you mean?

LC: That the words they're using, the metaphors that they're appropriating or transporting to a new place, end up being in some cases very fruitful and very productive, and that maybe this is happening without any conscious intent. I find that an interesting question to think about. Finding these associations between words and playing with them brings new insights. It's a form of making knowledge from serendipity almost, where you gather cases and put them together to learn new things. It's certainly one method I use as a historian, thinking my way not only with words but also through words, and I wonder if that might be a useful and a different way to talk about what it is that scientists do.

SR: I thought about it less in terms of science, although obviously rhetoric studies and discourse analysis show the extent to which metaphors are embedded in scientific practice. From my own work, I'm really interested in how constructing new kinds of words—neologisms but also wordplay—can itself be a kind of theoretical work. One thing that wordplay does is level the playing field between theory and empiricism. Rather than describing the world as it is and then just dropping some analysis on top—in which case theory comes second to the description of the world as it "really" is—theorizing is actually the work one does, which not only shapes the world, but is also something that the historical actors one writes about are doing, and which, as an anthropologist, the people I write about are doing. They're analyzing and theorizing along with us! This produces what some scholars have referred to as lateral thinking, and here I'm thinking of Bill Maurer and Stefan Helmreich in particular. What this means is that, as historians or anthropologists, we're working with the same theories but maybe talking about them or shifting them a little bit. We're all engaged in the same kind of concept-work.

LC: So, if I return to the question I asked earlier about creation and construction, would that be a way to tap into this approach? How have you seen those words being deployed and used in synthetic biology in your fieldwork?

SR: I have a good story about that from when I was first doing research in a synthetic biology laboratory. It's about a lab meeting I attended, and in the lab meeting there was a first-year graduate student who was very nervously giving a presentation for the first time. He described this virus they were working on. They were redesigning the virus, streamlining its genome, taking bits of genetic material out to see how much they could remove and still have a viable virus, which, of course, is already complicated because viruses are only marginally alive. He started a sentence by saying, "Well, you know, what we intended when we created this virus..." and it was immediately apparent that he had made a huge social faux pas, because people who hadn't been paying attention instantly stopped what they were doing.

And I turned to look at him. Suddenly, the room went completely quiet and the principal investigator of the lab said, "We don't create, we construct." At the time, I was totally confused about what had just happened, but I have since realized that refusing the language of creation was a way of trying to argue against intelligent designers. This may seem somewhat counterintuitive, but many believers in intelligent design were very excited about synthetic biology, because they thought that if scientists at MIT are having a hard time designing life, then obviously life couldn't have arisen spontaneously—life must require an "intelligent designer." So, in an effort to distance themselves from creationism or intelligent design, these MIT synthetic biologists completely eradicated the word "create" from their vocabulary.

LC: That's interesting. I often have historical echoes that spring to life in my mind when I hear stories like this from the present day. I think of the horticulturist Luther Burbank from the end of the nineteenth century in California; he bred new kinds of fruits and flowers and tried to produce novel, useful products, such as white blackberries and spineless cactuses and things like that. He produced a catalogue where he sold these new things, calling them "new creations." Calling them that was inviting trouble and he soon found himself invited to a church service, seated in the front row as a guest of honor, only to be harangued for the next forty-five minutes for having created these new types of flowers that God surely could not have intended. This seems to tap into that deeper, longer history of this concern with that word in particular.

SR: Right, absolutely! I wanted to get back to what we were saying before about the etymology of "demonstrative" and monsters. I was thinking, since we're talking about construction as a fourth, supplemental mode of reasoning, we could first touch upon abduction, which was the last of the three modes of scientific reasoning that Peirce initially outlined. If deduction means drawing logical conclusions from formal principles, and induction maps roughly onto the process of observing particular phenomena in order to abstract a more general rule or hypothesis, then a mode of reasoning that we haven't talked about yet is abduction—theorizing about the present by reference to a future. The monster is perhaps an example of abductive reasoning, because it represents a form pointing toward a potentially catastrophic future about which one is supposed to respond in advance.

LC: But maybe one could argue that, in the twentieth century, the "monster" becomes the "mutant."

SR: Certainly, yes, especially in the context of the laboratory. The mutant is the monster; the monster is the mutant. I'd think that monsters have better theological resonances than mutants, though. However, the notion of the abductive made me realize that abduction has many meanings. We've already talked about monsters; maybe it's time to talk about aliens.

LC: "Time to talk about aliens," I like that. Okay. A different form of abduction, and because I'm from New Mexico, I'll be happy to serve as the expert in this!

When we talk about the biological implications of aliens, I think about *The Andromeda Strain,* the 1969 Michael Crichton novel about a satellite descending to the American Southwest with a bug from space that, according to one full-page advert in the *New York Times* in 1969, caused "the world's first space-age biological emergency." This novel ended up playing a hugely significant role in discussions about the potential biohazards of genetic engineering and new work with recombinant DNA at the time; our laboratory safety protocols emerged in part out of concerns about planetary protection and germs from space. Crichton credited the idea for the novel, which was written while he was still in medical school, to a suggestion made in a seminar by the paleontologist George Gaylord Simpson, who had spoken about airborne microorganisms high in the Earth's atmosphere.

Simpson himself had lived in New Mexico for many years, and he'd had several heated arguments about the prospects of finding life on other planets. With his tremendous knowledge of paleontology and the role of contingency in the history of life on Earth, he derided those who felt that there might be humanoids "out there" somewhere—a term that had just been imported from science fiction—and even memorably called exobiology, a new science, "a science without a subject."

However, at the same time, we should also think of Julian Huxley—whose brother Aldous wrote *Brave New World* in the early 1930s and framed New Mexico as the place of savages, the last reservation free from the implementation of the new dystopian eugenics. Aldous was critiquing Julian's enthusiasm for eugenics, and also, in keeping with era, his brother's sense that the prospects for biology were almost limitless and that we might find ourselves some day in the position of being the "business managers" for evolution! There's a whole other metaphor floating around there. Being a business manager is different from being a god... and it is different from being a scientist!

SR: Much less fun.

LC: Yes, well, Julian Huxley thought it was interesting. But then again, he was one of the founders of UNESCO, so he liked administrative work. He engaged with the idea of space itself being a space to think about the futures of life, of how we might encounter it somewhere else, or of what might be necessary for us to travel elsewhere. J. D. Bernal, another figure from around that time, wrote a book, published in 1929, called *The World, the Flesh and the Devil*. He named the book after the three enemies of the rational soul that we needed to overcome: by "world" he meant we needed to leave the Earth; by "flesh" he meant that we needed to deliberately intervene into our own human germ plasm and radically transform ourselves for a future in space; and by "devil" he meant we had to learn how to deal with our desires and our fears, our imaginations and our stupidities.

These were the different things to think about in considering what the future of humans in space might be like. There's lots of talk, and we've already covered some of it today, about what life in space might be like, or life elsewhere, and so maybe it's worth exploring how that story connects with the story here on Earth.

Maybe I can return to an earlier thread then: One of the experts in mutation in the first half of the twentieth century was Hermann Joseph Muller, who figured out how to use ionizing radiation to create mutant fruit flies. He became very concerned about the effects of radiation from nuclear testing, but also thought that his studies of radiation-induced mutation could provide insight into how life might have emerged in other places and how we might manage to escape Earth, if we need to at some point in the future. There was kind of a wonderful red thread that bound "life as it could be": both his using radiation to produce new life forms—and he succeeded in doing that!—and his figuring out how life might be elsewhere. As it turns out, he had been a mentor to Carl Sagan. Muller and Sagan read lots of science fiction. They even went to science fiction conferences together. When Muller was sixty-eight, Sagan was twenty-three, and a very unusual friendship was established between them. It turned out that in his lectures Muller had often talked about chromosomes as the threads of destiny, as red threads—the threads we should pay attention to in a larger cord of the history of life on Earth.

He used to like to imagine geological time as an extended thread, with every yard or meter being 10,000 years. And he'd say that, at any given time, at any cross section of the thread, the amount of all the germ plasm or genetic material on Earth would be the size of an aspirin. This germ plasm was the most important stuff in the world, he felt, and in a world full of nuclear testing, we needed to protect it from the effects of radiation.

Last year I discovered that Muller had even received a birthday card from Carl Sagan in 1955 that said "the red thread slowly weaves its way upwards," with an image of Mars—the best one they had available at the time—and a diagonal red thread across it... It took me a while to figure out that this was Carl telling the story *back* to Joe of how the history of life on Earth was a narrative we should think about extending to outer space as well.

What I love about this story is the instability in the meaning: Is it we should *take* life there or is it life *is* also there?

SR: That is astonishing.

LC: But the thread is also lost because we don't know how to understand it.

SR: Right, so there's the thread of germ plasm, of life beyond Earth, of the origin of life on Earth, as well as planetary and evolutionary deep time–it really is astonishing.

LC: Arguments about contingency and determinism also fit into that. Would life emerge in the right circumstances if given the chance? Could life emerge in many different ways and in many different places? These have remained questions for a long time.

SR: It's interesting that you bring that up because that's a question that my interlocutors in geobiology, who study the origins of life on Earth, are taking on. They're also influenced by Carl Sagan's thinking about astrobiology, but more so by Lynn Margulis, who worked in geobiology and developed the theory of symbiogenesis. Specifically, Margulis showed that eukaryotes emerged when prokaryotes cooperated with one another. More broadly, Margulis brilliantly demonstrated that cooperation is at least as important to survival as Darwinian competition. But as I travel with geobiologists to various field sites, I realize they're all sci-fi fans. And one of the books that they've recommended to me is this odd novella called *The Dechronization of Sam Magruder.*

LC: That book was recommended to you? It was unrecommended to me by somebody as an example of one of the worst science fiction books she had ever read...

SR: Oh, it's horrible!

LC: Because the person who recommended it knew her paleobiology, I thought, well then, I have to read it. I had to know what's so bad.

reduce

witch

SR: It's a terrible book! The author is none other than George Gaylord Simpson, an invertebrate paleontologist, and one of the giants of his generation in Earth and Life Sciences. The novel was published post-humously in the 1990s, though Simpson likely drafted it sometime in the late 1970s.

> LC: Interestingly, I read a letter the other day in which Simpson had received a new manuscript from London just when he was heading back home, and he was going to be reading Lynn Margulis' work. There's another genetic connection right there, in that Margulis' work is being commented on by this paleontol-ogist thinking about these issues.

SR: Absolutely.

> LC: And I'm sure there's a science fiction novel included in there somewhere, too.

SR: I'm sure had Margulis written a science fiction novel, it would have been great! But no, Simpson did. It's quite interesting, though, because he's trying to think about planetary deep time. And the best way he can find to do so is by writing a time-travel story, in which this person, clearly a thinly veiled version of Simpson himself, acciden-tally travels between time quanta and lands, I think, in New Mexico at the end of the Cretaceous, if I remember correctly. It's right around the K-T (now K–Pg) boundary... and so he kind of whiles away his time.

> LC: The only man in the world...

SR: Eating turtle eggs and carving fieldnotes into sand in the hopes that someday they will be fossilized, and sixty million years in the future someone will read his fieldnotes, which would have since fossilized in sandstone.

> LC: If I'd seen them in amber at the Smithsonian, I'd definitely have wanted to read them!

SR: What I find most interesting about this is the mode of reasoning, this attempt to inhabit deep time and try to understand what it is and how life might have developed in form, deformed, transformed across deep time. This requires a mode of thinking that most of the time we might consider highly unscientific and speculative. We could in fact describe it as abductive! I think in this sense there is a speculative way of reasoning about life and time that is very much genetically a part of scientific reasoning.

LC: And you see it very clearly in a book where he writes himself into the story.

SR: Right.

LC: If I remember right, you've probably read it more recently than I have, it is the loneliness that he talks about of being the only man in the world and then thinking about whether he should help these little mammalian things to get to the next stage of evolution or not, and if there's anything that can be done. There is both this speculative, imaginary traveling back in time and putting himself in that position, but also having the character then consider whether he has an obligation to undertake some sort of constructive action to accelerate evolution, even when one is thinking over millennial time spans.

SR: Right. That is an interesting point. We were talking about abduction and the abnormal and the monstrous and that got us to storytelling. One way of posing a question about this is to ask what the place of storytelling is in thinking about the relationship of life to form, both in theories of the origins of life in the lab and on Earth, but also of life elsewhere.

LC: I think coming up with a convincing narrative is obviously part of interpreting the evidence, part of convincing oneself that one has made sense of something. You can do that in many different forms: in formal scientific ways; in thinking a way through fiction; by imagining oneself in a certain place to be able to make those connections. Yet it's interesting to think about the fact that these stories are written in private, are shared and circulated, then read and used as ways to think. We should think of them as equivalent to laboratory notebooks: that they are other tools used to construct these realities.

SR: What do you mean?

LC: We sometimes want to make distinctions around those stories or elements that have been proven or accepted, right, and that's what the *real* story is. But, in fact, it's these larger frameworks that might actually be the operative thing that gets one to want to experiment in the first place—or that gets one to think about how to frame something so that it becomes more convincing. When I think about the radium story, which I mentioned earlier, it's a narrative of the early Earth being billions of years old and having a more radioactive early environment. If one has that narrative in mind, then one can imagine the experiment that would complete it or to bring it to pass.

SR: So, in this regard, storytelling is actually reasoning before the fact.

LC: Right, storytelling is reasoning before the fact, that is, wondering if this or that is a future we could bring about.

SR: Yes, I agree. It's a way of trying to imagine life otherwise, because it's a way of trying to remove one context and plug in another one and then see what stays the same and what doesn't. It is an experiment with form, taking these long spans of time and trying to spin them out to see what happens. How does form change over time? It's a way of delaminating from multiple contexts, both with regard to Earthly contexts but also with regard to the time in which we find ourselves.

LC: And what ways can there be to that imaginative process of exploring the life space of possible forms of life? I'm reminded of an astrobiology conference a couple of years ago where they asked—and they were analogizing to the Cambrian explosion—can we imagine "new continents" of biodiversity, "where we are totally unconstrained by the lineages that preexist in nature"? Just as with all forms of biodiversity that emerged and exploded at a certain moment in time, we might be at a moment

now where we are constructing just such an explosion and bringing it about ourselves. There's a lot to analyze about the rhetoric
of the justifications happening there. But I think that analogy
between something that happened in deep time and the logical
possibilities of how life might be, even in very simple systems of
what we might do, begins to suggest not only that in the astronomical universe there are these infinite possibilities for life, but
that there might be astronomical possibilities within the com-
putation. As we extend our knowledge far beyond those combinations that we might be familiar with here on Earth, while
space might hold astronomical possibilities for life, life holds
astronomical possibilities within itself.

Further Reading
Luis Campos
    —*Radium and the Secret of Life*. Chicago, IL: University of Chicago Press, 2015.
    —"Life as It Could Be," in Kelly Smith and Carlos Mariscal (eds), *Social
    and Conceptual Issues in Astrobiology*. Oxford: Oxford University Press,
    2020, pp. 101–14.
    —"Strains of Andromeda: The Cosmic Potential Hazards of Genetic
    Engineering," in Campos, et al. (eds), *Nature Remade: Engineering Life,
    Envisioning Worlds*. Chicago, IL: University of Chicago Press, 2021.

Sophia Roosth
    —*Synthetic: How Life Got Made*. Chicago, IL: The University of Chicago Press,
    2017.
    —Turning to Stone," *Res: Anthropology and Aesthetics*, vol. 69 / 70, special
    issue: Writing Prehistory (Spring–Autumn 2018), pp. 62–75.
    —The Shape of Life," *Aeon* (March 15, 2018), https://aeon.co/essays/the
    -shape-of-life-before-the-dinosaurs-on-a-strange-planet, last accessed
    February 22, 2021.

Where Is Technology?

An interview about
governance and the division between
life and nonlife

Ana Guzmán: When you talk about the division between life and nonlife in your anthropological work, you often clarify the distinction with examples of objects, like fossils, which are divided into specific categories. In this context, you also criticize how the social relations that make this division and organize these categories are neglected. My question relates to whether the distinction between life and nonlife goes beyond aesthetics; whether there is recognition of something being linked to the terms and conditions of perception. How does the notion of agency come in here, which is not necessarily trapped within, let's say, the division of space?

Elizabeth Povinelli: This question takes us to technology and artistic practice. I'm a member of the Karrabing Film Collective. Other than me, the collective is composed of Indigenous families from the north-western coast of the Northern Territory of Australia. There are many reasons why we make films, and the installations that sometimes accompany their screenings in galleries and museums. One of the reasons we make them is to refuse to be governed according to settler imaginaries; another reason is to reinforce the joy of remaining governed by what Karrabing believes is a proper and right way of looking at existence. Therefore, the primary audience of the films (and the practice of making the films) is the entire array of human and more-than-human agencies that define Karrabing existence—agencies that don't abide by the divisions between life and nonlife, but rather flow across them. We've been thinking of our work as "art for the ancestors" and our aesthetic practice (a practice of shaping the senses, perceptions, and concepts of the human and more-than-human world) as beginning and ending in the world Karrabing hold, and seek to extend, across generations.

One of the clips from the film we made touches on the question of technology, artistic practice, agency, and the reinforcement of Karrabing analytics of existence; it goes into the pleasures of being

governed by something else. The clip is from our third film, *Wutharr,
Saltwater Dreams*. It's the first one we created entirely by ourselves,
without anyone from outside the group. We've never used a script or
storyboard, even in the first two films that involved a small non-Karr-
abing crew (cinematographer and sound). We have a basic idea about
the film, but where it actually goes just depends on who shows up
and what happens. But for our third film we decided we would do the
shooting according to the rhythms of local time, using iPhones and
shooting when people wanted to shoot rather than when an outside
crew was available.

Wutharr is based on a true story about a boat that broke down. Actually, it is an amalgamation of two events, because the boat broke down
twice. I was in the boat when it first broke down. We were stranded
on the south side of a vast harbor (Anson Bay), where there are no
human settlements. A handful of us had hopped off the boat to look
for a waterhole in a swamp we had heard about—we wanted to see if it
stayed wet through the long northern dry season. The rest of the group
sailed down the coast to go fishing. As night was coming down, we
looked hopefully on the horizon for the boat because we knew, once
the sun set, hordes of mosquitoes would emerge from the swamps. You
have no idea how a wall of mosquitoes that thick can emerge at night
there—you never want to know. You open your hand and swing it in the
air and you have a handful of these human-eating machines.

When we were recreating this moment, we placed a bunch of us
on the beach, sitting around apprehensively, as we were. One of the
older men, Rex Edmunds, hears a crow, he looks up, and says, "That's
not a good sign." Next to Rex is a young man, Ethan, who is lying on
the sand, flicking the sand with a little piece of dried grass. This is
something we do when we're bored, and I think he was actually bored
by the shot. He's like, "What time is this scene going to end?" Then
I brought my phone really close to his hand, exploring, digging, and
flicking the sand. In the image, you can see that the ground is sandy
on top and then there are ashes below where he's flicking.

So, in this one little scene we have three forms of techne—the technology of the phone, the technology of the piece of dried grass, which
is used as a stick, the technology of the crow's call: All are wrapped
into each other and raise a question as to why the boat might not
have returned, if you know what they all mean. Ethan's use of the
piece of grass to probe the sand reveals an even older technology, fire,

underneath, so we know that everyone's ancestors are there; these are the ashes of their fires. We know when a crow sits next to you cawing it means "something is wrong."

We have technology (fire; crow's call) that has left behind a sign (ashes; sound pattern), which serves as a technology for interpreting what happened to a boat. We recreate this with another technology (iPhone hardware and software) and edit it using yet another technology. The eventual outcome being that when we look at what Ethan was doing because he was bored during the shooting, it is no longer about boredom but about the pleasures of finding your history in the moment of making it, thus rewriting a different archive of the ancestral present. Now, where's technology, where's life, where's nonlife? Why do these distinctions matter? What work do they do? What work is done when you erase the distinction? I think this is what Karrabing is trying to figure out.

> AG: Going further, how you recognize something as life or nonlife is not only a question of aesthetics, nor is it only political, it is also epistemological. The distinction between life and nonlife relates closely to the question of form, and that distinction, which drives the process of knowing something as life or nonlife, is not neutral.

EP: Yes, absolutely, these distinctions are saturated with governance. Again, it is important to point out that even if you go to the belly of the beast—Western technoscience and their sustaining onto-epistemologies—even they know that the distinctions they make between life and nonlife, organic and synthetic, ancestral pasts and presents, are artificial. One can only define life from within the border of its membrane or skin analytically. In reality, that membrane must be open, must be unfurled into a space far away from it. In other words, biologists know what we describe as life cannot be defined simply from what I call its membrane or skin. We say a cell has a membrane. We have a membrane, called skin. Population geneticists might say a species has a membrane. The skin of the species is its ability to transfer genetic material sexually. From a biological perspective, we can say that the membrane is what allows a living organism to survive in the habitat in which it evolved. The skin is something that we say protects something until you puncture it and thereby kill it.

But if the membrane defines the difference between life and milieu, how distended is this difference, how many membrane folds does it take for it to be external to the organism, to be its milieu, or just how far into life can the milieu fold before it ceases to be itself? I use the simple example of breathing—and the differential access to non-toxic air.

Breath cannot be cut into life and nonlife/the epistemological and the political. The toxic particulates produced by extractive and consumptive capital are formed in a political formation as surely as they are reformed and recirculated in an environmental formation. The pollution of Black, Brown, and Indigenous lands goes hand in hand with police violence towards Black, Brown, and Indigenous bodies that gave rise to the Black Lives Matter political organization around "I Can't Breathe." The sealing of individual life in the imaginary of a self-organized body and destiny is epistemologically and politically psychotic.

> AG: I know names are not all that matters, but I am curious about the kinds of entities we're dealing with. Bruno Latour, for example, put forward the idea of Gaia not as a subject but as a kind of agent. How would you name the agency and non-separation in the geontopower—the governance of life and nonlife—form of understanding? Or would you say, "No, let's not name it, let's just say it's a form of existence?"

EP: We are now witnesses to a number of movements, most notably beginning in Bolivia, in which people are extending human rights to what were called natural formations, or nature, many under the name of Gaia. These movements seek to decenter the human—a particular kind of human, the type that has benefitted from this division, that is, a white, European human, in its colonial forms as well. As Denise Ferreira da Silva's work suggests, the extension of the human comes with risks. We might ask: Where are the natural formations of so many colonized lands?

I myself have imagined W. E. B. Du Bois walking along the boulevard in the 1920s or 1930s—which he did—knowing like everyone about the sadisms of King Leopold's actions in the Congo, talking about the reduction of life to bare life and the reduction of nonlife to nothing. I sometimes imagine what Du Bois thought about the sadisms and the illnesses of those Europeans walking along those streets. How somehow they could separate their own good life from what was going on in the Congo and didn't see the things they were standing on—the rocks, granite, marble, copper—as having been torn out of a form of existence upon which their sadistic treatment of others was built.

Du Bois could be seen as a critical forebear of what I am calling geontopower: looking at the monsters who thought rock was nothing but something for them to stand on, and that other humans were nothing but things from which they could extract. When I use the concept of geontopower, I'm trying to understand how this division between how you think about, how you treat, how you visualize this division, this fundamental division, lies at the root of producing the kinds of human monsters who have closed their eyes to the interdependent relations of existence. This way of avoiding merely looking but also acting, allows certain kinds of questions and ethics and social relations and differential treatment. As First Nation theorist Glen Coulthard has argued, colonialism didn't just dispossess people of their lands, it dispossessed, or tried to dispossess, an entire entanglement of relations between particular humans and their more-than-human world.

Now, to get to your question directly, no, I would not name it. Instead, I am interested in a certain syntax between what I am calling the four axioms of existence that inform an increasingly large space in some parts of critical theory. I expect most people will recognize these axioms.

The first axiom is the claim that existence is entangled, and by that theorists don't mean that there's a thing and a thing or a subject and another subject or subject and object that are tied together, rather, they mean that the conditions of being are only this-ish, here-ish because the condition of any being is in that-ish and over there-ish. For example, for me to exist as the kind of thing I am, I need air to be composed in a specific way. Or, if I want to breathe unpolluted air and want to be able to purchase cheap commodities then I need the air pollutants produced in the manufacturing products to remain somewhere else, say in China. So my consumer health is over there in an increasingly toxic China.

The second axiom is often narrated as if it were the logical result of the first axiom. Because existence is entangled, we see a differential power to affect the entanglement regionally or globally. The first axiom provides the ontological setting, and the second axiom elaborates and situates it in actual social worlds. If you're living in a poor part of Mexico City, then no doubt you will probably be living closer to a concentration of industrial toxins. Numerous scholars have documented how poor Brown, Black, and Indigenous communities carry an unequal burden of environmental pollution. This burden is the result of the historical ways that geosocial space has been entangled in structures of racism and colonialism. And this burden results in these communities having less power to affect how they are entangled.

The third has to do with the nature of the political event. Now, we don't just focus on the big events like the catastrophe, but small events, the poverty and the quasi-events, and we also don't think about eventfulness at all, we think about thresholds, so that always just being sunk in toxicity, or always just not quite being allowed to, that's the effort you're bringing up, having to work more.

The fourth is then provincialization of Western epistemologies and ontologies, which is what we've been talking about. Again, the only reason we should care about any of this is that we seek to reorganize the entanglement so that the direction of value-extraction stops going one way, and the entire modality that allows extraction value—reduction to bear life, and so on—stops being the system. In other words, should we care what existence is in the abstract and as a first principle before "adding" on sociology/anthropology (axiom two) and then politics (axiom three)? Is axiom four the culmination or the starting point? I try to take a firm position and say, I don't care what existence is in the abstract. I care, apropos of axiom four, that the entanglements which arose from axiom four created the epistemologies and ontologies that support it as well as the specific entanglement of extractions and accumulations. Okay, so what do we call that? What do we call those? What do we call this? Some people say Capitalocene, some people say capitalism, some people say colonial capitalism.

AG: Some people say Anthropocene.

EP: I can't say Anthropocene, for reasons that I talk about in *Geontopower*. I can't say Gaia either, because it makes it the Earth, in a way... Again, Latour is careful to say, "I'm not talking about Mother Earth,

I'm talking about how we think." Yeah, I know. However, again, these names are focal points, these names are practices of approach, these frames, and the names are practices of attention. Yes, of course, we want to pay absolute attention to those people who have been telling the colonial world for hundreds and hundreds and hundreds of years—through pre-capitalism and then capitalism and then whatever this post-capitalism is—that this division and hierarchy of being is not only simply wrong but also dangerous, and will lead to the unravelling of our existence. Of course, we want to pay attention to that, but Gaia's not going to do that, we need names that foreground colonialism, racism, and capitalism.

This text is a shortened and lightly edited transcript of a conversation between Elizabeth Povinelli, Anthropologist and Professor at Columbia University, and Ana Guzmán, a former research assistant at the Haus der Kulturen der Welt, Berlin, hosted by Reece Cox at *Info Unlimited* on Cashmere Radio. The full episode can be found at https://cashmereradio.com/episode/info-unltd-with-elizabeth-povinelli-and-ana-guzman-3/.

What and Whom Are We Working For?

A conversation about diasporic existences,
translating between cultural contexts, and political
engagement in academia

Kaushik Sunder Rajan: There are three potential points of departure
from which to figure out what this question is about. The first is in
the question "what are we working for?" itself: Who is the "we" here?
The second relates to your work on the implicit subject of the norm
that we are thinking of when we're thinking about these questions:
is there one? And the third is: What is the conjuncture of our conversation, from which we're addressing this question, individually and
together? Where are we speaking from at this moment, individually
and collectively? Maybe it would be interesting, Maria, just to start
by talking about what you're working on right now and what you're
thinking about?

> Maria Chehonadskih: My research focuses on the epistemolo-
> gies of socialism. I have been working with Soviet revolution-
> ary archives since I moved to the UK in 2013. Soviet archives are
> strange places to be, problematic places. I have to say that this
> "place to be" has been conditioned by the very fact of moving
> from Moscow to London. The necessity to introduce, mediate,
> translate unpronounceable names and "exotic" concepts, and,
> above all, to construct a relationship between the unpronounce-
> able and the established has determined my attempt to recon-
> figure conceptual coordinates and academic canons of Marxist
> thought. I have never felt that my work is a local or regional artic-
> ulation of a conceptual difference, but this is how it is perceived
> in the academic context. A naive universalism, or rather the
> naive assumption of Marxism as universalism, vanishes as soon
> as the geopolitics of knowledge is considered. "This place to be"
> is problematic because it is a structurally designated position
> given to anybody who moves from one geopolitical and cultural
> space to another. An Iranian is going to write about Iran, a Chi-
> nese person is going to write about China. Whatever the original
> intention is, this place performs the function of the represen-
> tation of a certain difference. This is a structural designation

of identity that one must carry, along with an accent and a visa in your passport. That is one danger of such work in the multinational English-speaking context. Thus, my struggle with this problematic position is double coded: to engage with marginalized traditions and to write transversally (not nationally or universally). For the broadly speaking Anglophone community of researchers, for whom Cold-War narratives about these archives remain unquestioned, it is also a kind of counternarrative.

There is also something that I want to stress. At the beginning of my research, when I was a PhD student, I operated freely with a wide range of ideas and concepts of both Soviet and international origin. I thought they equally worked to answer my research question, which at the time had to do with the problem of proletarianization and precarity. However, it became apparent to me that a certain kind of epistemological resistance exists in the Soviet-era works. Soviet texts are not applicable to the capitalist reality, because they were meant to engage with the problem of socialism and communism in an actual historical situation. This does not mean that they are utopian or speculative to the point of absurdity. It is a misleading characterization typically imposed by scholars who cannot decipher the epistemic code of revolutionary archives. My favorite example of such confusion is an episode from Andrei Platonov's anti-Stalinist novel *The Foundation Pit*, depicting the meeting of a bear and the party bureaucrat Pashkin.[1] This bureaucrat wants to find and promote the poorest worker in town. Local workers suggest that it is a class-conscious blacksmith's apprentice who works the longest shifts and is the best shock worker[2] in town. However, neither Pashkin nor the reader knows that this worker is not human, but a bear. When Pashkin finds out, he thinks that the workers ridicule him. In this way, the storyteller directs the sympathy of the reader to the conformist Pashkin, for whom a bear cannot be counted as a worker. This episode grounds a number of surrealist interpretations ranging from the exoticization of the Russian bear figure to the representation of these

1   Andrei Platonov, *The Foundation Pit*, trans. Robert and Elizabeth Chandler and Olga Meerson. New York: NYRB Classics, 2009, pp. 107 f.
2   *Udarnik* (shock worker) was an accolade given to a high-performing worker.

workers as slaves or beasts. Yet the bear is as real for the working-class characters of this novel as it was for the Voronezh region at the beginning of the 1920s. The biographer of Platonov found out that there was a real bear-blacksmith, who worked at one of Voronezh's suburban smithies, and the writer saw this bear many times. For Platonov, what the bear does in the smithy is more important than who he is—a human or an animal. In the peasant and proletarian experience, the working-class bear or the "class conscious horse" is not a surrealist fantasy. If we abandon the point of view of the party bureaucrat, we can see how Platonov expands the Marxist understanding of labor and exploitation. He introduces the concept of laboring animals, plants, and the natural environment.

The more I was engaging with the Soviet revolutionary archives, the less I was sure that it is enough to simply have a knowledge of Russian or a certain cultural connection with it. The connection one ideally should have is an experience of the post-revolutionary time. My favorite work that grasps the strangeness and absolute otherness of an epistemic configuration is Foucault's *The Order of Things*.[3] This is how I think we should read socialism in order to understand what it was. If you will, the most difficult task for us, living one hundred years after these events, is to penetrate the mental space of the post-revolutionary society. This relates to the question of "who are we?": We are those who live in the post-socialist and postcolonial world. Any segment of this world, as a post-Soviet space, is characterized by historical amnesia and an inability to engage with traumatic events, such as Stalinism, for example. Political confusions and social disorientation have roots in that history. I think this might be familiar to many postcolonial authors to some extent. Even beyond theory, one can see this in cinema or in art. In the Philippines, for example, there is a similar question of how history is erased and how one can narrate it again.

3   Michel Foucault, *The Order of Things: An Archaeology of the Human Sciences* [French 1966]. New York: Pantheon Books, 1970.

KSR: What you are describing is familiar to postcolonial authors, yes. Regarding the question of "what are we working for" and who is the "we," it's very interesting to me that you began your account with the fact of your immigration to the UK; you began your account with its being that of a diasporic academic. I think that's very familiar to post-colonial authors, and it's certainly very familiar to me. The mediations and translations that are required not just to make sense *of* the materials of one's objects of study (which, in your case, reside in the place you came from), but also to make sense *to* one's metropolitan interlocutors, who might well be invested in difference but who have too often already constructed that difference, epistemically, on their own terms. I believe that this necessitates a deconstructive reading of the material that one cares about. It begs the question: Who are we translating to and who are we translating for? And, as you point out, the language politics of this are of course important.

Yet, while the problem-space of diasporic translation that you outline is familiar to me, the specifics of the kinds of translations that you need to make are no doubt quite different. In my work, I deal with generally Anglophone postcolonial contexts in both India and South Africa (both places, of course, with many languages and complex language politics). But this question of always feeling like one is... how do I put this?... there's this odd disjuncture where being a part of the metropolitan university—an elite, private American university, in my case—gives me certain kinds of intellectual and political protection that certainly don't exist in the Indian university today, where friends, colleagues, comrades, students are literally being attacked legally and physically for acts of thinking, speaking, teaching, and writing. Mine is thus an incredibly privileged place from which to think about certain kinds of political matters, the privilege of stepping out of the set of politics in order to think about it, and to step into what is in many ways a depoliticized space, even though of course the American university has its own politics. At the same time, it's vexing because I always feel like I'm mediating and translating to groups of people who don't get what is obvious to the people that I want to be accountable to, if that makes sense. So it's very interesting for me to see what the starting point of certain conversations can be in India and South Africa. There, one can start a conversation with the colleagues and comrades one is speaking to with the presumption of imperialism and know that there is a shared historic sense of what that means.

It's actually very hard to talk about imperialism in the US and get any kind of genuine understanding of it. So I spend most of my time trying to explain what it is. That question of what we are working for, I think, raises particular kinds of issues for the diasporic scholar, including the diasporic scholar who is in a privileged position. It's not a position of marginality, but of what Homi K. Bhabha would call hybridity. A question of always crossing borders, always switching codes, such that even the classroom is always partially an alien space. It's a question of, as Gayatri Spivak has put it, learning how to be "outside in the teaching machine."[4]

This leads directly, indeed, to Spivak's question of what it means to teach in the metropolitan university out of that subject position, which includes teaching students who themselves are also quite substantially diasporic and who therefore come from their own conjunctural situations, their own sets of conversation, their own accountabilities, many of which have to be variously disguised or even shelved in order to gain professional recognition or legitimacy. I think it leads to some very interesting epistemic and methodological challenges that are political works of translation. So, what are we working for in theory, in practice, and also in teaching?

> MC: I think it's very interesting what you said about the diasporic academic and the elite universities. I think I would reverse it slightly, because for my generation, we are more like nomadic academics. Over the last five years since the completion of my PhD, I've worked in very different places across the UK. In the West Midlands, some of my students were almost illiterate; they had problems with writing. Then I came to Oxford as a post-doc, and this is a very different context with very different students. In the middle of that, I also worked at an art academy in London, which is an upper to middle-class environment with many international students from elsewhere. I think this creates two things: First of all, academic commitments are so fragmented. You cannot establish one type of relationship with, or even politics of, teaching. You may be given four different modules to teach. You

4   Cf. Gayatri Chakravorty Spivak, *Outside in the Teaching Machine*. London: Routledge, 1993.

create

trap

will not even choose what these modules should be about and what kind of literature you can suggest to your students. You are going to mark about seventy essays per term, and this inhuman labor will lead you to treat this work as another poorly paid, precarious job on a market. You would seek to find time and space to engage with politics and life outside of the university. What we miss in this context is what Alexander Bogdanov called a "labor of generations."[5] The chance to develop and build on ideas from generation to generation is lost in the context of fragmented, precarious labor and managerial orientation toward trends. In the UK, entire departments and disciplines disappear. The restructuring of jobs and constant cuts destroy what has been achieved after years of collective work and research. The very possibility of socially reproducing ideas is threatened.

KSR: Maybe I can say three sets of things in response to this, Maria. (In the third I will come more specifically to some of my own current work and thinking.) First, I find your phrase "nomadic academics" really interesting, and I see what you mean by that. I think that, personally, I am more resolutely a diasporic academic than a nomadic academic, as I've been in one institution for ten years. But more directly, and with regard to this conjunctive moment, I self-consciously inhabit a diasporic space, because I became an American citizen after Trump was elected in 2016—more than two decades after moving to the US—because it no longer felt safe or responsible to live in this country as a non-citizen. It felt irresponsible not to vote, so it was a very self-conscious act of throwing myself into liberal representative political democracy, which I found myself believing in and fighting for quite seriously over the past few years. Second, what you've pointed to is a cultural fragmentation, but my own diasporic inhabitation of the American university doesn't presume belonging to a broader Indian diasporic community in the US in any way (often,

---

5   Alexander Bogdanov, *Elementy proletarskoi kul'tury v razvitii rabochego classa. Lektsii prochitannye v Moskovskom proletkul'te vesnoi 1919 goda* (The Elements of Proletarian Culture in the Development of the Working Class. Lectures Delivered at Moscow Proletkult in Spring 1919). Moscow: Gosudarstvennoe izdatel'stvo, 1920, pp. 48 f.

indeed, quite the contrary). The politics of that diaspora is quite complicated, certainly the Indian diaspora of my class position being quite substantially pro-Modi, for instance. There's a whole set of things that are not indicative of my community of practice.

The thing I want to emphasize is your statement that, in the process of nomadic or diasporic itineraries, one sees the fragmentation of academic commitments. I think that's right, and I see that as a very serious issue in the US as well. Here, I think the fragmentation is happening along two axes: One is that the differentiations and hierarchies among different types of American universities have become violently visible during the time of the pandemic. Just the everyday labor of academic reproduction is radically different depending upon whether one is in a private university or a public university, or whether one is teaching in a community college (which have been completely snowed under). Depending on where your money comes from, radically different kinds of precarity and stability are being made evident in ways that I think directly impact the everyday lives of teachers and students in different ways. The universities are in crisis, in the US as it is elsewhere, but that crisis is manifesting in extremely differentiated ways. The second axis of fragmentation is generational, given the precarity of the times and the shrinking of the academic job market for non-precarious labor. Our students, graduate students in particular, have to treat their studies and research as training for a job, not as preparation for a vocation. I wasn't trained that long ago, but I was trained to treat teaching as a vocation and it's very, very hard to know how to responsibly teach a generation that is forced to think of something as a job when one has an ethical commitment to a vocation. These disjunctures between ethos and political-economic reality manifest in all sorts of unpredictable ways.

So, this question of who our students are is one that I don't know how to answer at this moment. What are we working for, or who are we working for? That's very direct. I know in a formal institutional sense who I'm working for, but I don't necessarily know—in the still emergent disjunctures between pedagogical ethos and professional pragmatics—who my student is. What kind of knowledge worker am I training or am I supposed to train, to what ends?

MC: I wanted to say that the way you identify this conflict between vocation and job is a personal existential drama for me.

I always wanted to be a university teacher. The role of teacher seemed the most ethically acceptable in this ugly, capitalist world. It's the least horrible thing you could do. Unlike being a debt collector or a big corporation manager, you would definitely do less harm to society. But these reflections were a product of different contexts. Back in Russia, all the universities are extremely defunded, and your role is truly civic and vocational. Only a social commitment would bring you to the university system, but at the same time, an experience of severe poverty may drive you out too. Yet even if managerialism, corporativism, and algorithmic segmentation of work determines academic labor in the UK, most of us want to be teachers and researchers for the same reason. It is the least horrible and one of the most socially engaged forms of work. When I was teaching somebody else's syllabus, I had to go through the text of a reactionary British philosopher. I had no option of replacing his work with something else, even though I attempted to. Half of my students were Black and Brown, but I had to teach an obscure thinker who developed very problematic ideas approaching the worst examples of nationalism and homophobia. My approach was to read it with a harsh criticism. You still try to change things even with what you have. This example shows that academic labor is obviously not just a job. I agree that vocational and civic commitment is absolutely essential. To challenge a curriculum is a generational dialogue. You pass this challenge from teacher to student. A teacher–student generational dialogue is a transmission and reproduction of a critical standpoint and a style of thought.

KSR: I think it's gratifying to me that we've ended up with this question of civic responsibility, because one of the things I was thinking about during the past year of getting involved in some small way with this last election, was that the word "civics" is a word I have never heard used in the twenty-three years I've lived in the US. Yet it played such a central part in my foundational political formation. I had my first copy of the *Communist Manifesto*, which was a Soviet publication of course, in the 1980s when I was twelve. But my first influence regarding education in politics was in school, my ninth standard civics textbook. It was written by Sudipta Kaviraj, now one of the foremost political theorists of India, teaching at Columbia.[6] He had written a school textbook, and it was transformative for me because it talked about things like representative democracy and political parties. What it was really talking about was an ideal of India that was grounded in political modernity. It's been interesting to see how difficult it is to translate the kind of ethos that such a textbook embodied—from another time and another place—to the American classroom today. It's quite difficult because the sort of epistemic milieu in which I grew up in India, which of course was always contentious and argumentative and full of critiques of political modernity as well as the developmentalism that it entailed, nonetheless treasured the inheritance of political modernity as potentially socially transformative, albeit always in need of an anti-colonial radicalization. The origin story of that political modernity was granted in all sorts of aspirations for social transformation. It's quite hard to translate that investment, which still animates my sense of the political in both my research and my teaching, in the American university today. It is blocked of course by the neoliberal, corporate, financialized institution that the university has become, but it also often seems unintelligible to my colleagues on the American left. We have come full circle to where you started this conversation, Maria: the question of "who do we work for?" as one that is not just a question of the historical conjuncture of the contemporary research university, but also one of our varied diasporic presences within it. Outside, within the teaching machine.

6   Cf. Sudipta Kaviraj (ed.), *India Constitution and Government: A Textbook in Civics for Classes* 9 *and* 10. New Delhi: National Council of Educational Research and Training (NCERT), 1997.

+   Katrin Klingan is a literary scholar, curator, and producer
of art and cultural projects. Since 2011 she has been a curator
at the Haus der Kulturen der Welt, where she heads the Department of Literature and Humanities. In this capacity, she has
developed and realized parts of *The Anthropocene Project*
(2013–14) as well as the long-term research project *Anthropocene Curriculum* (since 2013) which explores, in an experimental
manner, new forms of knowledge. Klingan's recent projects
at HKW include *Mississippi. An Anthropocene River* (2018–19),
Life Forms (2019), and *The Shape of a Practice* (2020).

+   Nick Houde is a researcher for the long-term projects
Anthropocene Curriculum (2013–present) and *Technosphere*
(2015–19) at the Haus der Kulturen der Welt. Outside of HKW,
Houde has taught at various schools in Europe, including Bard
College Berlin, Zurich University of the Arts, and the University
of Applied Arts in Vienna, and is lead investigator for the Vertical
Union Working Group at the research- and network-platform
Trust. Formerly, he has written articles, given public lectures,
and performed music under various monikers.

+   Johanna Schindler is a postdoctoral researcher at the
WÜRTH Chair of Cultural Production at Zeppelin University,
Friedrichshafen, the managing editor of the *Journal of Cultural
Management and Cultural Policy*, adjunct lecturer at the Uni-
versity of Connecticut, and a freelance translator and editor.
Previously, she has worked as a researcher and coordinator of
the project *Technosphere* (2015–19) at the Haus der Kulturen
der Welt, Berlin.

+   Luis A. Campos is Associate Professor and Regents' Lecturer in the History Department at the University of New Mexico. He serves as Secretary of the History of Science Societ. Trained in both biology and the history of science, Campos' scholarship brings together archival discoveries with contemporary fieldwork at the intersection of biology and society. He is the author of *Making Mutations: Objects, Practices, Contexts* (2010), Radium *Radium and the Secret of Life* (2015), and *Nature Remade: Engineering Life, Envisioning Worlds* (2021).

+   Maria Chehonadskih is a philosopher and critic. She is a Max Hayward Visiting Fellow at St Antony's College, University of Oxford. Her research and work concentrate on Soviet epistemologies across philosophy, literature, and art, as well as on post-Soviet politics and culture. As part of her Max Hayward Visiting Fellowship, she is working on her book *The Science of Organization: Transformation of Knowledge after the October Revolution*.

+   Reece Cox is a Berlin-based artist, writer, and music maker. Cox explores cultural contexts and formats of representing sound and other time-based media. He produces a monthly program called *Info Unlimited* on Cashmere Radio wherein he hosts conversations and listening sessions with artists working in a variety of media.

+   Ana Guzmán thinks about the logical conditions for the intelligibility of nature. Her research interests go from the concept of life in German idealism to reproduction theories and sex toys.

+   Hao Liang—having studied at Sichuan Fine Arts Institute—lives and works in Beijing. For him, practicing Chinese painting is more than a journey that unites technique and life experience—it is also a reflection on the individual exploration of one's relationship with the world. His recent solo and group exhibitions include *Hao Liang: Circular Pond* (Aurora Museum, Shanghai, 2019), *Hao Liang: Eight Views of Xiaoxiang* (Ullens Center for Contemporary Art, Beijing, 2016), the 57th Biennale di Venezia

(Venice, 2017), and *Streams and Mountains without End: Landscape Traditions of China* (Metropolitan Museum of Art, New York, 2017).

+ Hu Fang is a fiction writer and art critic based in Guang-zhou, China. He is co-founder of Vitamin Creative Space. His writings explore the forms and meanings of contemporary living. His books in English translation include the short story collection *Dear Navigator* (2014), and *Towards a Non-intentional Space* (2015), an essay book reflecting on the research pro-cess of the "Mirrored Gardens" designed by Japanese architect Sou Fujimoto.

+ Elizabeth A. Povinelli is an anthropologist and filmmaker. She is Franz Boas Professor of Anthropology at Columbia University, New York, and one of the founding members of the Karrabing Film Collective. Povinelli's writing has focused on developing a critical theory of late liberalism that would support an anthropology of the otherwise, unfolded primarily from within a sustained relationship with Indigenous colleagues in north Australia. Her recent publications include *Geontolo-gies: A Requiem to Late Liberalism* (2016) and an upcoming graphic essay, *The Inheritance*. Povinelli lives and works in New York and Darwin.

+ Sophia Roosth is an anthropologist who writes about the contemporary life sciences. In her book *Synthetic: How Life Got Made* (2017), Roosth asks what happens to "life" as a con-ceptual category when experimentation and fabrication converge. Grounded in an ethnographic study of synthetic biologists, she documents the profound shifts biology has undergone in the postgenomic age. She is currently a Cullman Center Fellow at the New York Public Library.

+   **Kaushik Sunder Rajan is Professor of Anthropology and co-director of the Chicago Center for Contemporary Theory at the University of Chicago. His work engages social theories of capitalism, technology studies, and postcolonial studies, holding a special interest in the global political economy of biomedicine, with a comparative focus on the United States and India. He is the author of** *Biocapital: The Constitution of Postgenomic Life* **(2006) and** *Pharmocracy: Value, Politics, and Knowledge in Global Biomedicine* **(2017).**

Colophon

Das Neue Alphabet (The New Alphabet) is a publication series
by HKW (Haus der Kulturen der Welt).

The series is part of the HKW project *Das Neue Alphabet*
(2019–2022), supported by the Federal Government
Commissioner for Culture and the Media due to a ruling
of the German Bundestag.

Series Editors: Detlef Diederichsen, Anselm Franke,
      Katrin Klingan, Daniel Neugebauer, Bernd Scherer
Project Management: Philipp Albers
Managing Editor: Martin Hager
Copy-Editing: Mandi Gomez, Hannah Sarid de Mowbray
Design Concept: Olaf Nicolai with Malin Gewinner,
      Hannes Drißner

Vol. 7: *Making*
Editor: Katrin Klingan, Nick Houde, Johanna Schindler
Coordination: Niklas Hoffmann-Walbeck
Contributors: Luis Campos, Maria Chehonadskih, Ana Guzmán,
      Hao Liang, Hu Fang, Elizabeth Povinelli, Sophia Roosth,
      Kaushik Sunder Rajan
Translation: Melissa Lim
Graphic Design: Malin Gewinner, Hannes Drißner, Markus Dreßen
Type-Setting: Hannah Witte
DNA-Lettering (Cover): Kay Bachmann
Fonts: FK Raster (Florian Karsten), Suisse BP Int'l (Ian Party),
      Lyon Text (Kai Bernau)
Image Editing: Scancolor Reprostudio GmbH, Leipzig
Printing and Binding: Gutenberg Beuys Feindruckerei GmbH,
      Langenhagen

Published by:
Spector Books
Harkortstr. 10
01407 Leipzig
www.spectorbooks.com

Distribution:
Germany, Austria: GVA Gemeinsame Verlagsauslieferung
      Göttingen GmbH & Co. KG, www.gva-verlage.de
Switzerland: AVA Verlagsauslieferung AG, www.ava.ch
France, Belgium: Interart Paris, www.interart.fr
UK: Central Books Ltd, www.centralbooks.com
USA, Canada, Central and South America, Africa:
      ARTBOOK | D.A.P. www.artbook.com
Japan: twelvebooks, www.twelve-books.com
South Korea: The Book Society, www.thebooksociety.org
Australia, New Zealand: Perimeter Distribution,
      www.perimeterdistribution.com

Haus der Kulturen der Welt
John-Foster-Dulles-Allee 10
D-10557 Berlin
www.hkw.de

Haus der Kulturen der Welt is a business division of Kultur-
veranstaltungen des Bundes in Berlin GmbH (KBB).

Director: Bernd Scherer
Managing Director: Charlotte Sieben
Chairwoman of the Supervisory Board: Federal
      Government Commissioner for Culture and the Media
      Prof. Monika Grütters MdB

Haus der Kulturen der Welt is supported by

 Minister of State
for Culture and the Media

 Federal Foreign Office

First Edition
Printed in Germany
ISBN: 978-3-95905-465-2

Recently published:
Vol. 1: *The New Alphabet*
Vol. 2: *Listen to Lists!*
Vol. 3: *Counter_Readings of the Body*
Vol. 4: *Echo*
Vol. 5: *Skin and Code*
Vol. 6: *Carrier Bag Fiction*
Vol. 7: *Making*

Forthcoming:
Vol. 8: *Looking at Music* (June 2021)
Vol. 9: *A Kind of World War* (July 2021)
Vol. 10: *Re_Visioning Bodies* (August 2021)
Vol. 11: *What Is Life?* (September 2021)

Vol. 8:   *Looking at Music*
Editors: Lina Brion, Detlef Diederichsen
Contrib.:   Stefanie Alisch, Peter Kirn, Mari Matsutoya,
            Adam Parkinson, Terre Thaemlitz, TOPLAP
ISBN: 978-3-95905-492-8
            June 2021

The performance of computer-produced music has broken with the codes of the concert: The audience can no longer watch music being created; the causal relationship between gesture and sound has been cut. With laptop performances, a format has emerged in which the audience stares at people staring at screens. *Looking at Music* asks: What role does visibility play in the experience of music? How important is the live character to the future of music performance? Screen views at "algo-raves" or virtual reality stars like Hatsune Miku reintroduce visual stimuli on different levels; in kuduro, the musical focus is on the dance expertise—whilst other musicians have long left the stage-centered spectacle behind.

Vol. 9:   *A Kind of World War*
Eds. / Text: Anselm Franke, Erhard Schüttpelz
ISBN: 978-3-95905-494-2
            June 2021

Aby Warburg's famous lecture on the Hopi snake ritual in Arizona
is one of the most commented art history transcripts of the
20th century. But while Warburg's essay is firmly anchored in
the canon of art history, to a wider public—especially in Europe—
little is known about its source, the snake ritual and its history.
A Kind of World War is dedicated to what Aby Warburg largely
ignored himself: that not only the ritual, but also the images
of the ritual—to whose global distribution Warburg contributed—
have a political history. The volume seeks to demonstrate that
Warburg's art history, insofar it outlines an internal history
of the European psyche, must be read in conjunction with its
external counterpart, the history of colonization, war and cultural
entanglement.

Vol. 10:   *Re_Visioning Bodies*
Editor: Daniel Neugebauer
Contrib.:   Maaike Bleeker, Ayşe Güleç, Carmen Mörsch,
            Eliza Steinbock
ISBN: 978–3–95905–496–6
            July 2021

This volume plunges into a number of different archives and resurfaces with physical techniques: Eliza Steinbock finds love in the Lili Elbe Archive, Europe's largest collection of trans* and queer history; Carmen Mörsch describes how bodies that act as a medium for artistic expression communicate more than just art, inviting us to take a discrimination-wary view; Ayşe Güleç opens up an archive of migrant melancholia and speculates on stories that have ended in failure due to systemic racism. Maaike Bleeker slips into the role of Neo in *The Matrix* and plugs a data-transfer cable into our spinal cord to ask how intellectual knowledge and physical knowing condition one another.

Vol. 11:   *What Is Life?*
Editors: Stefan Helmreich, Natasha Myers, Sophia Roosth, and Michael Rossi in associatian with Katrin Klingan and Nick Houde
Contrib.:   Stefan Helmreich, Natasha Myers, Sophia Roosth, Michael Rossi
ISBN: 978-3-95905-498-0
             August 2021

"What is life?" is a question that has haunted the life sciences since Gottfried Treviranus and Jean-Baptiste Lamarck independently coined the word "biology" in 1802. The query has titled scores of articles and books, with Erwin Schrödinger's in 1944 and Lynn Margulis & Dorion Sagan's in 1995 being only the most prominent ones. In this book, the editors curate and speculate upon a collection of first pages of publications from 1829–2020 containing "What Is Life?" in their titles. Replies to the question—and, by extension, the object of biology—have transformed since its first enunciation, from "the sum of the functions that resist death" to "a bioinformation system" to "edible, lovable, lethal." Interleaved are frame-shifting interruptions reflecting on how the question has been posed, answered, and may yet be unasked.